SPOTLIGHT ON EXPLORERS AND COLONIZATION™

FERDINAND MAGELLAN

First Circumnavigator of the Earth

SUSAN MEYER

ROSEN PUBLISHING®

New York

Published in 2017 by The Rosen Publishing Group, Inc.
29 East 21st Street, New York, NY 10010

Copyright © 2017 by The Rosen Publishing Group, Inc.

First Edition

Library of Congress Cataloging-in-Publication Data

Names: Meyer, Susan, 1986– author.
Title: Ferdinand Magellan : first circumnavigator of the Earth / Susan Meyer.
Description: First edition. | New York : Rosen Publishing, 2017. | Series:
  Spotlight on explorers and colonization | Includes bibliographical
  references and index.
Identifiers: LCCN 2015051394| ISBN 9781477788011 (library bound) | ISBN
  9781477788004 (pbk.) | ISBN 9781499438031 (6-pack)
Subjects: LCSH: Magalhães, Fernão de, –1521—Juvenile literature. |
  Explorers—Portugal—Biography—Juvenile literature. | Voyages around the
  world—Juvenile literature.
Classification: LCC G286.M2 M49 2017 | DDC 910.92—dc23
LC record available at http://lccn.loc.gov/2015051394

Manufactured in the United States of America

CONTENTS

4   THE WORLD BEFORE MAGELLAN

6   EARLY EUROPEAN EXPLORATION

10   SPAIN VERSUS PORTUGAL

12   FROM A PORTUGUESE FARMHOUSE

14   A LOVE OF TRAVEL

16   TO INDIA AND BEYOND

20   A NEW GAME PLAN

24   TURNING TO SPAIN

26   SETTING OUT TO MAKE HISTORY

28   TROUBLE IN SOUTH AMERICA

32   THE STRAIT OF MAGELLAN

34   THE WIDE, BLUE PACIFIC

36   THE JOURNEY ENDS

40   MAGELLAN'S LEGACY

42   GLOSSARY

43   FOR MORE INFORMATION

45   FOR FURTHER READING

46   BIBLIOGRAPHY

47   INDEX

THE WORLD BEFORE MAGELLAN

Today, people know a great deal about Earth's geography. Most people can picture and sketch the continents and oceans. We know that Earth is vast. In fact, it has a circumference of 24,901 miles (40,074 kilometers).

Imagine a time before people had this information. In Europe, in the fifteenth and sixteenth centuries, people were just beginning to learn the size of the world. Some people believe that geographers at this time thought that the world was flat and that explorers would sail right off the edge if they weren't careful. That is actually a misconception. Most Europeans knew that the world was round. What they didn't know was how long it would take to travel around it.

Brave explorers set out to sea, not knowing when they would see land again or what and whom they would encounter when they did find it. One of these explorers was Ferdinand Magellan. He planned and led the first expedition to circumnavigate, or sail around, the globe. In doing so, he would transform maps, explore a whole new ocean, and further connect the gaps between Europe, the New World, and Asia.

Ferdinand Magellan was an intrepid explorer who sailed thousands of miles in his lifetime, under the flags of both Spain and Portugal.

EARLY EUROPEAN EXPLORATION

At the end of the fifteenth century, people in Europe were excited about exploring the rest of the world. One of the main reasons for this exploration was to find faster routes to Asia. Everyone wanted to get to Asia because spices grew there, in places like India and Indonesia. Many spices came from the Moluccas, a part of Indonesia often known as the Spice Islands. Spices had many uses in European food and medicine. However, they were very expensive. Arab traders controlled the spice trade and charged Europeans a lot of money for spices.

Nutmeg, which Europeans in Magellan's time used for flavoring and as a preservative, grows on trees native to the Banda Islands, in the Moluccas.

Many Europeans believed there was a route to reach the Spice Islands and the rest of Asia without going through Arab lands. They thought that instead of going east across the land, they could sail west across the ocean or go south around Africa. It was a gamble because at that time no one knew how far the ocean continued or what people might encounter. Two European countries in particular were very focused on finding and controlling a new route for opening the spice trade. These countries were Spain and Portugal.

Bartolomeu Dias led a Portuguese expedition around the perilous waters of Africa's southernmost point to reach the Indian Ocean.

Both Spain and Portugal built up large navies to try to control the seas. They put money into expeditions led by explorers, all hoping to find a route to Asia by sea.

Two Portuguese explorers tried sailing south, around Africa. The first was Bartolomeu Dias. In 1488, he became the first European to sail around the tip of Africa when he sailed past the Cape of Good Hope into the Indian Ocean. In 1498, Vasco da Gama made it one step further—sailing around Africa and arriving in Calicut, India. He was hailed as a hero back in Portugal. Da Gama was the first to successfully find a sea route to Asia.

In 1492, Christopher Columbus tried sailing west instead of south on behalf of the king and queen of Spain. He hoped to find a path to Asia across the Atlantic Ocean. Unfortunately, what people did not know then is that two huge continents—North America and South America—stand in the way. Columbus thought he had reached the Indies (part of Asia) in 1506, but he had really reached the Bahamas. He called the people he found there Indians.

SPAIN VERSUS PORTUGAL

As Spain and Portugal both learned more about the world, they both wanted control over it. By 1493, they nearly started a war over it. Luckily, the two countries were able to come to an agreement instead. They would divide the New World in half by drawing a line down the center of the map, through the Atlantic Ocean. This was called the Line of Demarcation. Spain would get all lands west of the line. Portugal would get all lands east of the line. Both countries agreed to not sail through the other's waters.

Pope Alexander VI first suggested this agreement in 1493. In 1494, the line was moved further west. This new Line of Demarcation was officially defined in the Treaty of Tordesillas. Because of this treaty, Spain was even more interested in exploring lands to the west. Around this time a young Portuguese government clerk named Ferdinand Magellan was beginning to develop an interest in exploration himself.

This engraving shows the establishment of the Line of Demarcation. Pope Alexander VI is the figure seated under the canopy on the left.

FROM A PORTUGUESE FARMHOUSE

The world into which Ferdinand Magellan was born was one at the beginning of some major changes. Magellan was born in either Sabrosa or Porto, Portugal, in 1480. His parents were Portuguese nobles who lived in a large farmhouse. Ferdinand was their third child. When Ferdinand was seven years old, he was sent to school at the Vila Nova de Mura. This was a school that was part of a monastery, or a home for monks.

Magellan's parents died when he was only ten. Because of his parents' noble background, the young Magellan was sent to serve the Portuguese royal family.

Young Magellan was sent to work in the court of Queen Eleanor of Viseu. She was the queen consort (meaning she was married to the ruling king) of Portugal from 1481 until 1495. This statue is of her.

He moved to Lisbon, the capital city of Portugal. In Lisbon, he served the queen as a page. In addition to doing errands for the queen, Magellan also continued his education in Lisbon. He learned reading, history, and math, as well as specific skills, like navigation, that would help him later in life.

A LOVE OF TRAVEL

Magellan's move to Lisbon would ignite in him a desire to see more of the world. The capital city was on the coast and the expeditions of great explorers such as Vasco da Gama had set sail from its busy port. This sparked an early interest in travel for Magellan.

He wanted to go out and see the world. He also hoped to put his navigation skills to the test. There were many expeditions leaving Portugal at this time, but Magellan had trouble joining one. Part of the trouble was that the king of Portugal, Manuel I, didn't like Magellan. No one is exactly sure

why this was, but it is possible he looked down on Magellan because he came from the country and because his family, while noble, was not rich.

Even though he did not have the king's favor, Magellan would soon get the chance to set out on his first voyage—not as an explorer but as a soldier.

TO INDIA AND BEYOND

In 1505, Magellan went to sea for the first time. He became a member of a two-thousand-person expedition to India that was led by the nobleman and explorer Francisco de Almeida. The fleet was sent to take over the sea routes in the Indian Ocean, so that Portugal could keep control of the spice trade.

Magellan sailed with the fleet along the coast of East Africa and then to India. In 1506, Magellan took part in several battles with ships from the Ottoman Empire (which today is Turkey). The Ottomans also wanted control of the spice trade. Through many battles, Magellan demonstrated bravery and skill as a soldier. He became a lieutenant.

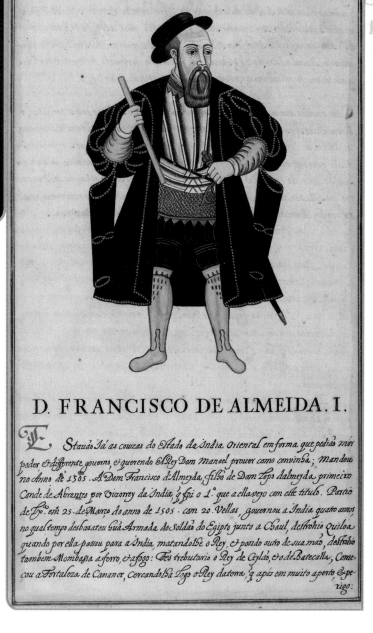

D. FRANCISCO DE ALMEIDA. I.

Staudo Ja as couzas do Estado da India Oriental em forma que pediao mei pader e differente governo, e querendo El Rey Dom Manoel prouer como convinha; mandou no Anno de 1505 . A Dom Francisco d'Almeyda, filho de Dom Lopo d'almeyda, primeiro Conde de Abrantes por Vizorey da India. q foi o 1.º que a ella veyo com este titulo. Partio de Lyo. em 25. de Março do anno de 1505 . con 20. Vellas, governou a India quatro annos no qual tempo desbaratou Sua Armada do Soldão do Egipto junto a Chaul, destrohio Quiloa queando por ella pasou para a India, matandolhe o Rey, e pondo outro de sua mão, destrohio tambem Mombaça a ferro, e a fogo: Es trebutario o Rey de Ceylão, e o de Batecalla, Começou a Fortaleza de Cananor, Cercandoiba Logo o Rey datorra, q após em muito aperto e perigo:

Then, in 1509, Magellan fought in the Battle of Diu. This was a sea battle in the Arabian Sea near the port city of Diu, India. In this battle, Magellan was very badly injured. It took him many months to recover, but as soon as he did, he was eager to go back to sea.

The Portuguese soldier
and explorer Afonso de
Albuquerque is known
for conquering Goa,
in India, in 1510. He
helped open up trade
routes to the East.

In June 1511, Magellan set sail with a fleet commanded by the general Afonso de Albuquerque. They sailed to what is now the country of Malaysia in Southeast Asia. Once there, the Portuguese fleet conquered the city of Malacca. This city was a major trading center.

Following the successful conquering of Malacca, Magellan returned to Lisbon in 1512. He thought he would receive a hero's welcome. Instead, he returned to find he was no better off than when he had left. His soldier's salary was reduced, and he was very poor. He had few rich friends or helpful connections. Manuel I still didn't like or support him. All Magellan wanted was to return to sea.

Magellan volunteered for one more military mission. This time the fleet traveled to Morocco. During the battle there, Magellan was badly injured yet again. He never fully recovered and walked with a limp for the rest of his life.

A NEW GAME PLAN

In the fall of 1514, Magellan returned to Lisbon yet again. He was injured from battle and hoping to raise money for an expedition of his own. His plan was to find a new way to reach the Spice Islands. He had come to believe that the Spice Islands might be closer to the New World than previously thought. At this time, Europeans were still exploring the "New World," which is what they called the landmasses we now know as North and South America.

Around this same time, Magellan began to study astronomy. He worked with a Portuguese astronomer named Rui Faleiro. Faleiro used science and study of the stars to learn more about the world. From their

This woodcut shows sixteenth century astronomers working with tools, including an armillary sphere and astrolabe. These tools could also be used for navigation.

studies, Faleiro and Magellan became convinced that the Spice Islands could be reached by sailing west as Columbus had tried in 1492. They also determined they would need to travel south to sail around South America.

This illustration dramatizes Balboa's discovery of the Pacific on September 25, 1513. He was the first European to arrive at the Pacific from the New World.

In 1513, a Spanish explorer, Vasco Núñez de Balboa, had traveled through Central America in what is now the country of Panama. He reported having seen a great ocean beyond it. He called it the South Sea, but today we know it is the Pacific Ocean. Magellan believed that by sailing across this ocean, he would be able to reach the Spice Islands.

Not only that, but Magellan also believed there was a strait that cut through the continent of South America. By traveling through this narrow waterway, he believed the expedition could reach the Spice Islands without having to travel all the way around South America.

It was a good plan, but not one that would be easy to achieve. Beyond the sheer length and difficulty of such a voyage, there was another problem. By traveling west to reach the Spice Islands, the explorers would be crossing the Line of Demarcation. They would be traveling through Spanish territory.

TURNING TO SPAIN

Magellan went to Manuel I and asked him for money to fund a voyage west to the Spice Islands. The king refused to help him. Tired of the continued rejection, Magellan decided to try his luck with a new king. He and Faleiro set sail for Spain.

They arrived in Seville, Spain, on October 20, 1517. They took their idea to Charles I, who was king of Spain at the time. Magellan and Faleiro offered to reject their home country of Portugal and swear their loyalty to Spain. Magellan even married a woman, Beatriz Barbosa, who lived in Spain but was of Portuguese background. He assured the king that they wouldn't face problems of sabotage from Portugal

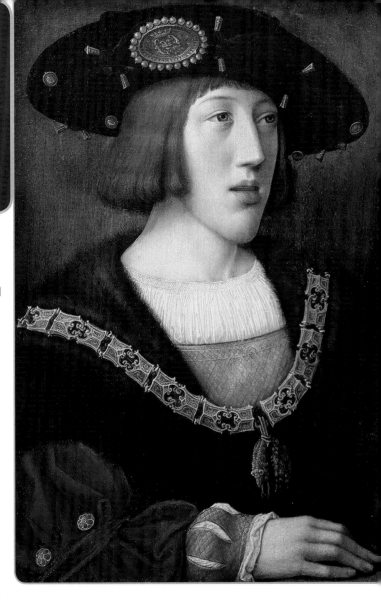

because they would be sailing through Spanish territory.

Charles I was only a teenager at the time. He liked Magellan and was excited by the idea of a western route to the Spice Islands. He was tired of seeing Portugal grow rich from the spice trade. He promised Magellan the money to fund the voyage and pay for a crew. He also promised Magellan some of the profits if Magellan was successful in his quest.

SETTING OUT TO MAKE HISTORY

On September 20, 1519, Magellan set sail with five ships and a crew of 270 men. Magellan sailed on his flagship, called the *Trinidad*. The other four ships were the *Santiago*, the *San Antonio*, the *Concepción*, and the *Victoria*. The ships were stocked with food, weapons, spare ship parts, and items to trade.

Magellan set the course south along the coast of Africa. He wanted to avoid any Portuguese ships because Manuel I had declared him a traitor. He expected people would assume he would be going straight west. While he did avoid attacks from

This engraving shows the *Victoria*. It was the only ship to survive the whole expedition and circumnavigate the globe.

Portuguese ships, he soon ran into other troubles. His ships faced harsh storms along the African coast.

He also faced trouble on board. Some members of the Spanish crew were not happy to follow Magellan. The Spanish captain of the *San Antonio*, a man named Juan de Cartagena, plotted against him. He wanted to murder Magellan and take over the expedition. Magellan was able to prevent the mutiny by binding Cartagena up in chains and keeping him below deck.

TROUBLE IN SOUTH AMERICA

Cartagena's mutiny would not be the last of the problems Magellan and his crew faced. As they turned west and crossed the Atlantic, they experienced periods of very little wind. Since their ships required wind to travel, this made for very slow going. They also faced blazing sun and many more storms. Their fresh food and water began to run out. Without access to fresh fruits and vegetables, the crew began to suffer from scurvy.

Finally, on December 13, the crew was overjoyed to see land. They landed in a bay, which is now Rio de Janeiro, Brazil. The

crew was greeted by the native Guarani people. The Guaranis were friendly, and the expedition traded with them for fresh food. The men rested and recovered. By Christmas, though, Magellan ordered them onward. They still had to travel south to find the pass that would take them to the South Sea (as the Pacific Ocean was known at the time). Magellan hoped that once they made it through this pass, it would be a short journey to the Spice Islands.

This lithograph shows Magellan confronting the mutinous crews of the *Victoria* and the *Concepción* after the Easter Day mutiny in 1520.

In January 1520, Magellan thought he'd found the strait. He sent the *Santiago* to explore. It was actually just a large river. The crew was becoming discouraged, but they sailed south, following the coast of South America. The weather became colder. They traveled through ice storms and freezing rain. Finally, Magellan realized they would have to stop. On March 31, they sought shelter in a bay in what is now Argentina. They planned to wait out the winter months, as winter in the Southern Hemisphere begins in June.

While stopped in Argentina, the crew again began to mutiny. On April 1, disloyal crewmembers took control of the *San Antonio*, the *Victoria*, and the *Concepción*. Magellan's ship, the *Trinidad*, and the *Santiago* remained loyal. Magellan was able to retake the mutinous ships. He killed the captains of the *Victoria* and the *Concepción* as a warning to the others.

In August, it was warm enough to leave Argentina. Only four ships remained. The *Santiago* had run aground in the Santa Cruz River. The other ships continued south.

THE STRAIT OF MAGELLAN

On October 21, Magellan and his four remaining ships entered a bay in what is now Chile. Magellan wasn't immediately sure that this was the strait for which he had been searching. He sent the *Concepción* and *San Antonio* ahead to see if the waterway continued. A massive storm hit. The ships were separated, and Magellan's own ship nearly sank. Luckily, the ships all survived the storm and reunited. Even better, they discovered that the waterway did keep going. Magellan named the pass the Strait of All Saints, but it would later come to be known in his honor as the Strait of Magellan.

However, just finding the strait was not the end of Magellan's travels. The strait itself was hard to navigate. It was full of rocky

This colored lithograph shows Magellan and his small fleet discovering the strait that would come to bear his name.

cliffs and narrow, winding paths. It took more than a month to get through it. During the journey, members of the *San Antonio* crew again mutinied. This time no one was able to stop them, and the ship sailed back to Spain. This left Magellan with only three ships and very low on supplies. Having rounded South America, he was now facing the wide Pacific Ocean.

THE WIDE, BLUE PACIFIC

Europeans had little knowledge of the body of water Magellan now faced. He called it the *Mar Pacifico*, meaning "calm sea," because it seemed to be less choppy than the stormy Atlantic had been. Magellan and his men would be the first Europeans to sail across the Pacific Ocean.

The expedition first reached the Pacific on November 28, 1520. Crew members hoped they were nearing the Spice Islands. They had no idea that the ocean they had just entered was the largest body of water on Earth. Through December and most of January, the crew would travel without ever finding inhabited land. Their food was nearly gone and their drinking water was

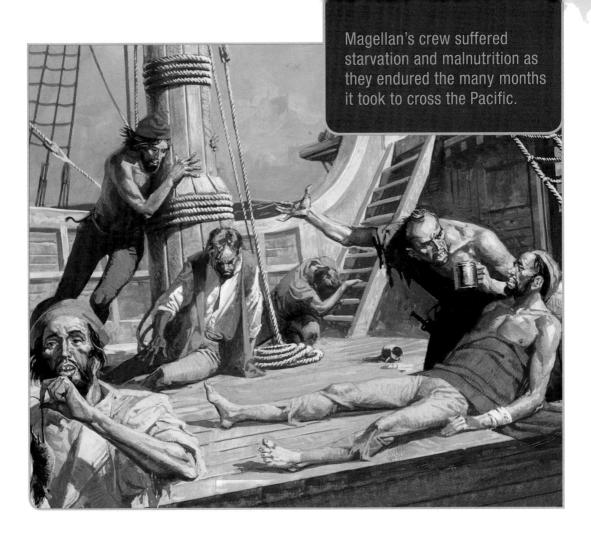

Magellan's crew suffered starvation and malnutrition as they endured the many months it took to cross the Pacific.

unclean. Some of the men died and were buried at sea.

On January 25, 1521, the ships reached a small island, where the men ate crabs and fish. On February 13, they crossed the equator. They continued west, always hoping the Spice Islands were just over the horizon. Finally, on March 6, 1521, they reached land with people on it. They had landed on Guam.

THE JOURNEY ENDS

Shortly after leaving Guam in early March, the expedition landed in the Philippines. Magellan spent many weeks on these islands. He tried to convert some of the native people to Christianity. During the voyage, Magellan had become more religious, perhaps because he had survived so many difficult situations. Whatever the reason, he seemed to lose interest in gold and the hunt for the Spice Islands. Now the most important thing in Magellan's mind was that everyone recognize and worship the same god that he did.

The leader of one of the islands, Mactan, did not want to listen to Magellan. Magellan

This mural shows the leader of the Mactan, Lapu-Lapu, about to deliver a fatal blow to Magellan.

was convinced that converting people to Christianity was the right thing to do and that those who did not listen should be punished. Many of his crew tried to talk him out of starting battles with the natives, but he would not be swayed.

On April 27, Magellan and sixty of his crew traveled to Mactan to try to punish the islanders for not obeying them. The Europeans were outnumbered. Wounded in the battle, Magellan died of his injuries.

While Magellan did not survive to see it,
the expedition continued on after his death.
The *Concepción* was destroyed because

The *Victoria* arrived in Seville, Spain on September 6, 1522, to much rejoicing.

there were not enough crew members left to sail three ships. The *Trinidad* and the *Victoria* continued sailing west. On November 8, 1521, they reached the Moluccas. After spending three months there, trading spices for the items on board the ship, the *Victoria* returned to Spain. It arrived back, full of expensive spices, on September 6, 1522, three years from when it had first set out. The ship had traveled 27,000 miles (43,452 km). Only seventeen of the original crew members were on board.

The *Trinidad* had left the Spice Islands with the *Victoria*. However, its crew was much smaller in number and very ill. The ship returned to the Spice Islands. The *Trinidad* didn't make its return to Spain until 1525.

The spices on board the ships ended up being worth just enough to cover the cost of the expedition. No profits or riches were made as Magellan had hoped. Nevertheless, the crew did make some incredibly important discoveries.

MAGELLAN'S LEGACY

Much of what we know about Magellan's incredible journey comes from one of his surviving crew members, Antonio Pigafetta. He assisted Magellan and kept a detailed journal of everything that happened.

Charles I would send other expeditions to try to repeat the journey Magellan had made, but none of them could do it. Magellan's bravery and determination had kept his crew together through mutinies, storms, starvation, and disease. His ability to navigate the treacherous strait that now bears his name was incredible in its own right. This waterway is considered difficult to cross even with modern navigation tools.

Although he died before seeing the completion of his dream, Ferdinand Magellan had a huge effect on the world. By circumnavigating the globe, his expedition proved conclusively not only that the world was round but also that the Atlantic and Pacific Oceans were connected. His voyage was the first to chart just how large the Pacific Ocean was. New maps were created to display this new knowledge. After Magellan, the world would never be the same again.

GLOSSARY

circumference The length of a line around a circle or the widest part of a sphere.

circumnavigate To travel all the way around something.

conquer To overcome by force.

convert To change the religion of a person or group of people.

expedition A journey made with a specific purpose, such as exploration.

flagship The ship carrying the commander of a fleet.

fleet A group of ships.

hemisphere Half of the earth.

inhabited Lived in by people.

lieutenant A military ranking.

mutiny A rebellion, especially on a ship.

navigation The science of plotting a course.

navies The ships and sailors that fight for countries on the seas.

page A servant who often delivers messages.

sabotage To intentionally cause something to fail.

scurvy A disease caused by a lack of vitamin C.

strait A narrow waterway connecting two larger bodies of water.

traitor A person who betrays his country.

treaty An official agreement between nations, often ending a war.

Mariners' Museum and Park
100 Museum Dr.
Newport News, VA 23606
(757) 596-2222
Website: http://www.marinersmuseum.org
This group of museums holds some of the largest
    collections of artifacts and historical objects on the
    exploration of the Western Hemisphere.

Maritime Museum
Praça do Império, 1400-206
Lisboa, Portugal
+351 21 362 0019
Website: http://museu.marinha.pt
Lisbon's Maritime Museum follows Portugal's long
    history of sea travel and exploration from the
    Age of Discovery onward. The exhibits include
    information on Magellan and his contemporaries.

Museo Nao Victoria
Magallanes y la Antártica Chilena Region
Punta Arenas, Chile
+56 9 96400772
Website: http://naovictoria.cl/?lang=en
The Nao Victoria Museum is an interactive exhibit
    in the Strait of Magellan about the history of
    Ferdinand Magellan. The museum includes

a life-size replica of the *Victoria* and features mannequins outfitted and armed in period dress.

National Maritime Museum
Park Row, Greenwich
London SE10 9NF
United Kingdom
+44 20 8858 4422
Website: http://www.rmg.co.uk/national-maritime
  -museum
This museum is the world's largest maritime museum and contains thousands of artifacts, maps and charts, and artwork related to exploration. Its website also includes background and biographical information on important explorers, including Ferdinand Magellan.

Websites

Because of the changing nature of Internet links, Rosen Publishing has developed an online list of websites related to the subject of this book. This site is updated regularly. Please use this link to access the list:

http://www.rosenlinks.com/SEC/magel

FOR FURTHER READING

Appleby, Joyce. *Shores of Knowledge: New World Discoveries and the Scientific Imagination*. New York, NY: W. W. Norton, 2013.

Charles River Editors. *Legendary Explorers: The Life and Legacy of Ferdinand Magellan*. Boston, MA: Charles River, 2012.

Connelly, Jack. *Ferdinand Magellan: Circumnavigating the Globe (Incredible Explorers)*. New York, NY: Cavendish Square Publishing, 2015.

Greenwood, Rosie. *I Wonder Why Columbus Crossed the Ocean: and Other Questions About Explorers*. New York, NY: Kingfisher, 2013.

Krull, Kathleen, and Kathryn Hewitt. *Lives of the Explorers: Discoveries, Disasters (and What the Neighbors Thought)*. New York, NY: Houghton Mifflin Harcourt, 2014.

Matthews, Rupert. *DK Eyewitness Books: Explorer*. New York, NY: DK Children, 2012.

Mundy, Robyn, and Nigel Rigby. *Epic Adventure: Epic Voyages*. Sydney, Australia: Kingfisher, 2011.

Oxlade, Chris. *Kingfisher Readers: Explorers*. New York, NY: Kingfisher, 2014.

Riffenburgh, Beau. *Mapping the World: The Story of Cartography*. London, England: Carlton Publishing Group, 2015.

When on Earth? New York, NY: DK Children, 2015.

BIBLIOGRAPHY

Bergreen, Laurence. *Over the Edge of the World: Magellan's Terrifying Circumnavigation of the World.* New York, NY: HarperCollins, 2004.

Guillemard, Francis Henry Hill. *The Life of Ferdinand Magellan and the First Circumnavigation of the Globe: 1480–1521.* London, England: Sagwan Press, 2015.

Kramer, Sydelle. *Who Was Ferdinand Magellan?* New York, NY: Grosset & Dunlap, 2004.

MacDonald, Fiona. *Magellan: A Voyage Around the World.* New York, NY: Franklin Watts, 1998.

Paine, Lincoln. *The Sea and Civilization: A Maritime History of the World.* New York, NY: Alfred A. Knopf, 2013.

Petrie, Kristin. *Ferdinand Magellan.* Edina, MN: Abdo Publishing Company, 2007.

Waldman, Stuart. *Magellan's World.* New York, NY: Mikaya Press, 2007.

INDEX

C

Cartagena, Juan de, 27
  mutiny of, 27, 28
Charles I, king of Spain, 24, 25, 40
Christianity, 36–37
Columbus, Christopher, 9, 21
Concepción, 26, 31, 32, 38–39

D

Da Gama, Vasco, 9, 14

E

expeditions
  to circumnavigate, 5, 41
  to India, 16
  Spanish and Portuguese, 5, 14
  to Spice Islands, 20, 23, 27, 29, 34, 36, 38, 39, 40

F

Faleiro, Rui, 20–21, 24
fleet
  conquering of Malacca, 19
  in the Indian Ocean, 16

G

Guam, 35, 36
Guarani people, 28–29

I

India, 6, 9, 16, 17

L

Line of Demarcation, 10, 11, 23

M

Mactan, 36, 37
Manuel I, king of Portugal, 14, 19, 24, 26
Moluccas, 6, 39
mutiny, 27, 28, 31, 33, 40

P

Portugal, 7, 9, 10, 12, 13, 14, 16, 24–25

S

sabotage, 24–25
San Antonio, 26, 27, 31, 32, 33
Santiago, 26, 31
Spain, 7, 9, 10, 11, 24, 33, 39
  Magellan and, 24–25
Spice Islands, 6, 7, 20–21, 23, 24, 25, 29, 34, 35, 36, 39
spices, 6, 39
  trade of, 6, 7, 16, 25, 39
starvation, 40
storms, 27, 28, 31, 32, 34, 40
strait, through South America, 23, 31, 32
Strait of Magellan, 32, 40

T

Treaty of Tordesillas, 11
Trinidad, 26, 31, 39

V

Victoria, 26, 31, 39

About the Author

Susan Meyer is an avid researcher of the great explorers and admires their personal sacrifices and willingness to spend months at sea. Meyer herself gets very seasick and would have jumped ship and gone searching for citrus at the first sign of scurvy. Meyer is the author of over fifteen children's and young adult nonfiction titles. She lives with her husband Sam and cat, Dinah, in Austin, Texas.

Photo Credits